Magic

HANDBOOK

CARD TRICKS

JOE FULLMAN

QED Publishing

Author Joe Fullman

Editor Amanda Askew

Designer Jackie Palmer

Illustrator Mark Turner for Beehive Illustrations

Publisher Steve Evans

Creative Director Zeta Davies

Contents

The magic of cards

Have you ever watched a magician perform an amazing trick and wondered how they did it? Then this is the book for you! Learn how to do 13 card tricks to entertain and astound your friends and family.

(1) Preparation

Sometimes you will need to prepare something beforehand to make a trick work.

(2) New Skills Alert

As you practise the tricks, you will learn several new skills, such as 'stacking the deck' and 'card peeking'. You will also learn 'sleight of hand' techniques, so you can move cards around without your audience seeing what you are doing.

(3) Difficulty rating

The tricks get harder throughout the book, so each trick has been given a rating. One is the easiest and seven is the hardest. The most difficult tricks will take a bit of practice to get right, but the results will be worth it!

Putting on a show

A good magician is more than just a skilled handler of cards. They should also be a storyteller and an entertainer. Props, such as a magic wand and glitter, can help bring a trick to life.

Forcing the card

The magician places a sealed envelope o table. They ask a volunteer to choose a The volunteer then opens the envelope. Sor the name of their chosen card has been wr on the piece of paper inside!

(1)

Preparation
You will need to 'stack the deck', so the third card in the deck is the Queen of Diamonds. Write the name of the card on a piece of paper, put it in an envelope and seal it. Place the envelope in your pocket.

(1) A hav car the pla to

(2) Give the deck of cards a quick 'false shuffle' and then hand them to your volunteer. Ask them to deal out the top six cards into two rows of three. The Queen of Diamonds should be in the top row on the right-hand side.

22

4) Skills needed...

The main skills you will need are explained the first time they are used in New Skills Alert.

The easier skills are explained on page 32.

- Card counting
- Card peeking
- Cutting
- Memory
- Observation
- Sleight of hand
- Spelling
- Stacking the deck

- Card forcing
- Double lift
- False shuffle
- Misdirection

5) Props needed...

The props you will need for each trick.

- A pack of playing cards, known as the deck. Each pack should contain 54 cards – two Jokers plus four suits of 13 cards. The suits are Spades, Clubs, Diamonds and Hearts.

- Envelope
- Elastic band
- Handkerchief
- Jacket
- Paper

- Pen
- Scissors (ask an adult)
- Shoe
- Toothpick or cocktail stick

NEW SKILLS ALERT

Card forcing

You can force someone to pick the card you want them to, whilst making it seem like they have chosen it at random! Once mastered, you can use this skill to make up your own tricks.

4 Ask your volunteer to pick two cards. If the volunteer picks the first two cards, remove them and the remaining card is their card. Go to step 7.

5 a) If your volunteer points to the first and the third card, remove the middle card. Go to part b.

6 a) If the volunteer points to the second two cards, remove the first card. Go to part b.

Top Tip!

Make sure the audience does not see you counting the cards, otherwise they may be able to work out how the trick is done.

The first magician

In the 1840s, the French watchmaker Jean Eugène Robert-Houdin became the first man to perform magic tricks in theatres in front of large audiences. His act featured several illusions that are still popular today, such as catching a bullet between the teeth and levitating.

▼ Jean Eugène Robert-Houdin is often called the 'father of modern magic'.

6) Stages and illustrations

Step-by-step instructions, as well as illustrations, will guide you through each trick.

7) Top Tip!

Hints and tips help you to perform the tricks better!

8) Famous magicians and illusions

Find out who are the most exciting and skilful magicians, and what amazing feats they have performed.

What better way to start than with the most famous magic word of all? Lay the cards out in the right way and 'abracadabra', you will have found your volunteer's card.

Skills needed...
* Card counting
* Spelling

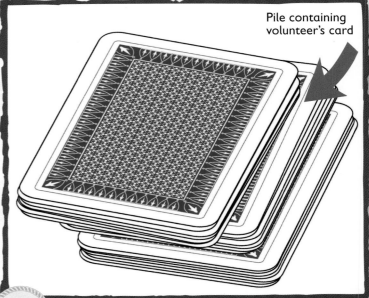

Pile containing volunteer's card

1 Deal 21 cards face up into three columns of seven cards. Ask a volunteer to choose one of the cards, but not to tell you which one. Instead, they should tell you which column their card is in. If they choose the eight of Diamonds, they would tell you that they had chosen column three.

2 Pick up the three columns, keeping the cards in the same order. However, make sure you pick up the column containing your volunteer's card second, so that it sits between the other two columns.

▲ Different countries use different styles of playing cards.

Card magic

The first cards for playing games were created more than 1000 years ago in China, which is where paper was invented, too. The playing cards that we use today were first made in Egypt about 700 years ago. Traders brought these cards to Europe, where they became very popular. Card games and tricks soon spread around the world.

3 Deal out the 21 cards again. Be sure to lay them left to right, rather than up to down. Ask your volunteer which column their card is in now.

4 Repeat step two, making sure you keep the cards in each column in order, and that you sandwich the column containing your volunteer's card between the other two columns.

5 Now deal the cards face down into a pile, spelling out the word 'abracadabra', saying a letter for each card you put down. When you get to the final letter 'a', hold the card in your hand. Ask your volunteer to tell you the name of their card. Slowly turn over the card in your hand to reveal their chosen card.

Hey presto!

Use the magic words 'hey presto' to find your volunteer's card. This trick is special because you do not touch the cards until the end of the trick. Your volunteer does most of the work, making it seem more magical.

Skills needed...
* ✳ Card counting
* ✳ Misdirection
* ✳ Spelling

1 Hand your volunteer a full deck of cards. Ask them to deal all the cards face down into two piles.

2 Ask them to choose one of the piles of cards and look at the bottom card, without letting you see what the card is. They must remember this card.

NEW SKILLS ALERT

Misdirection

For a trick to work, it is important that the audience does not see what is really going on. They should not spot the extra card hidden in your pocket or notice you taking a peek at the bottom card. To do this, magicians use a skill called misdirection – doing things that have nothing to do with the trick! You could tell jokes or wave a magic wand to distract the audience and direct them away from the secrets of the trick.

3 Your volunteer should put their chosen pile on top of the other pile and then square up the deck.

4 Ask your volunteer to deal the full deck face down into four piles. Ask them to look through each pile and tell you which pile contains their card.

Pile containing volunteer's card

5 Pick up the cards, putting the four piles back together to make a whole deck again. Be sure to place the pile containing your volunteer's card on top of the others.

6 Hand the full deck face down to your volunteer and ask them to start dealing out the cards face up. They should spell out the word 'presto', saying a letter for each card they put down.

7 Take the deck from the volunteer and turn over the top card. Hey presto, it's their chosen card!

Top Tip!

For step 5, use the new skill of misdirection. Perhaps you could wave a magic wand while you put the piles of cards on top of each other.

An Ace trick

Skills needed...
* False shuffle
* Memory
* Stacking the deck

With some card preparation, you can magically spell out the names of all the cards, from Ace to King.

Preparation

Before the trick starts, some of the cards need to be arranged into a certain order. This is called 'stacking the deck' and your audience must not see you do it.

The first 13 cards of your deck need to be in this order:
3, 8, 7, Ace, Queen, 6, 4, 2, Jack, King, 10, 9, 5

Make sure that the cards are in different suits. This will make it less obvious to the audience that the cards have been sorted.

1

When your audience is ready, give the deck a quick 'false shuffle'. This will make it look like you have changed the order of the cards, but will leave the first 13 cards in place, ready for you to begin the trick.

2

Announce to your audience that you are going to sort out the cards. Fan out the cards face up and show them to the audience. The cards will look like they are in a random order.

3

Count off the first 13 cards without changing the order and separate them from the deck. Then, fan out this pile to show the audience that they are in no particular order. Square up the 13 cards face down.

Fourth card is the Ace

Three cards are moved to the back

4 Tell the audience that you can find the Ace. Spell out the word 'Ace', taking a card from top of the pile as you say each letter and placing it at the back of the 13-card pile. Now turn over the next (fourth) card. It is an Ace! Place this face up on the table.

5 Next, spell the word 'two' out loud, taking a card off the deck for each letter and placing it on the bottom of the back. Turn over the next (fourth) card. It will be the two. Place this on top of the Ace face up on the table.

6 Continue spelling out the numbers and names of the cards. Each time, the following card will be the one you have spelt out, until you reach the King.

False shuffle

- Pick up the deck, as you would to do a normal shuffle.

- Rest the cards in the palm of your hand, with the backs of the cards pointing towards your thumb.

- Holding the cards loosely, take a pile from the middle of the pack, leaving the cards at the front and back.

- Drop the cards in small groups at the back of the pack.

- If you want to leave just the top card in place, pick up a large pile. However, if you want to leave several cards in place, pick up a smaller pile, between the middle and the bottom of the pack.

11

Mind reading

F or this trick, you will need to do a little acting. You are going to pretend that you have 'read the mind' of your volunteer. In fact, if you prepare the cards in the right way, this trick will work every time, without you having to do a thing!

Preparation

You will need to 'stack the deck' before facing your audience.

The first 11 cards need to be in this order:

6, 5, 4, 3, 2, Ace, Joker, 10, 9, 8, 7

If the cards are in different suits, the audience will not suspect that the cards have been sorted.

1 With your audience in position, give the deck a quick 'false shuffle' before you begin the trick to make it look like you have changed the order of the cards.

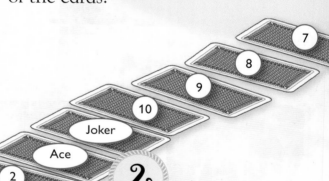

2 Lay out the first 11 cards face down in a row from left to right.

3 Ask your volunteer to move some of the cards from the right-hand side of the row to the left-hand side. They can move as many cards as they like, but they must be sure to move the cards one at a time.

4 Turn your back, so that you cannot see what your volunteer is doing. Ask them to tell you when they have finished moving the cards.

The first magician

In the 1840s, the French watchmaker Jean Eugène Robert-Houdin became the first man to perform magic tricks in theatres in front of large audiences. His act featured several illusions that are still popular today, such as catching a bullet between the teeth and levitating.

▼ Jean Eugène Robert-Houdin is often called the 'father of modern magic'.

5 Turn back and tell them that you are now going to reveal how many cards they moved. In order to make the trick appear more magical, ask your volunteer to think of the number of cards they moved. Tell them you are going to read their mind.

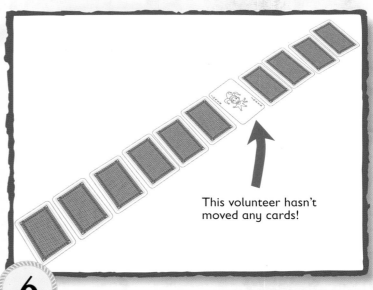

This volunteer hasn't moved any cards!

6 Count seven cards from the left and turn over the card. Whatever the number is on the card, that's the number of cards that have been moved. This works every time, no matter how many cards were moved. If the volunteer decided not to move any cards, you will pick up the Joker.

Top Tip!

Make sure the audience does not see you counting the cards, otherwise they may be able to work out how the trick is done.

Aces on top

volunteer thoroughly mixes up four piles of cards – but each pile ends up with an Ace on top. As long as your volunteer follows your instructions exactly, this trick will never fail. Make sure you do not forget which pile of cards is which!

Skills needed...
* False shuffle
* Memory
* Observation
* Stacking the deck

Preparation
You will need to 'stack the deck' before facing your audience. Sort through the cards, find the four Aces and place them on top of the deck.

1 Face your audience and give the deck a quick 'false shuffle' to make it look like you have mixed up the cards.

2 Hand your volunteer the deck of cards. Ask them to divide, or cut, the deck into four roughly equal piles. Remember which pile has the Aces in, or the trick will not work.

Move three cards to the bottom

3 Ask your volunteer to pick up one of the piles that *does not* contain the Aces. Ask them to take three cards from the top of the pile and to place them on the bottom.

4 Using the cards in their hand, they should then deal one card from the top of the pile onto each of the other piles. Then place the pile face down, next to the others.

5 Repeat steps 3 and 4 with another pile that does not contain the Aces.

6 Repeat steps 3 and 4 with the remaining pile that does not contain the Aces.

7 Repeat steps 3 and 4 with the pile that does contain the Aces.

Street magic

The magician David Blaine has performed many amazing tricks, including pushing a rolled-up dollar bill through a solid coin, levitating and even bringing a 'dead' fly back to life.

▼ David Blaine often performs tricks on the street to make the illusions seem more real.

8 Ask your volunteer to turn over the top card on each of the four piles. They are all Aces!

Magic elastic

U se the magical power of the elastic band to find your volunteer's card. For the best results, this trick should be performed in front of at least two people.

Skills needed…
* Misdirection
* Sleight of hand

Props needed…
* Elastic band

1 Put the elastic band in your pocket before the start of the trick. Shuffle the cards, fan them out face down, and ask your volunteer to take a card.

2 Ask your volunteer to show the card to the rest of the audience. Tell them that you are going to turn your back while they do this. With your back to the audience, you can now perform 'sleight of hand'. Turn over the pack so that the cards are all face up. Now turn over the top card so that it is face down.

Practise makes perfect

It takes practise and dedication to become a top card-trick performer. Dynamo is one of the UK's best young magicians. He is very skilled and makes his amazing card tricks seem effortless.

▶ Dynamo skilfully fans out a pack of cards during a trick.

3 Ask your volunteer to hide their chosen card. Turn back to face the audience. Now, take the elastic band from your pocket and wrap it around the deck widthways.

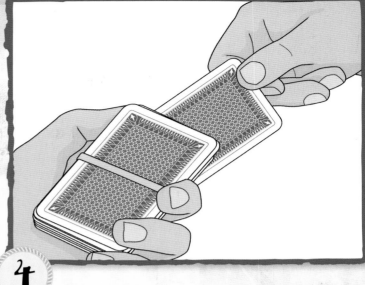

4 Holding the cards in your left hand with your palm facing upwards. Ask the volunteer to put their card face down into the centre of the pack.

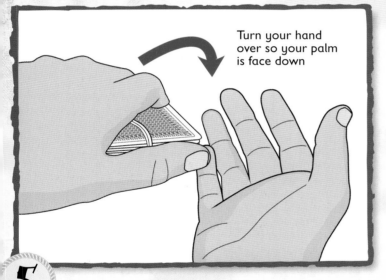

Turn your hand over so your palm is face down

5 Now you need to use the new skill of 'sleight of hand', so your audience does not see what you are doing. Pass the cards from your left hand to your right hand. As you do this, turn your left hand so that when it reaches your right hand, the palm is facing downwards.

6 Holding the pack in your right hand, ask the volunteer to twang the elastic band 'to make the magic work'.

Keep this card hidden

Volunteer's card

7 Place the cards back into your left hand – do not turn the deck over. Take off the elastic band. Fan out the cards in your hand until you reach your volunteer's card, which will be face up. Do not fan the cards all the way to the bottom or your audience will see that the bottom card is also face up, and may work out how the trick is done.

Odds and evens

Skills needed...
* Stacking the deck

No matter how many times your volunteer shuffles the cards, you always find their chosen card.

Preparation

You need to 'stack the deck' so that you have two piles of cards – one of even numbers, and one of odd. Jacks and Kings count as odd, Queens as even. The pile of odd cards will be slightly larger than the pile of evens. Place the pile of even cards on top of the pile of odd cards. Do not square the deck up, but keep the pile of even cards at a slight angle so you can see where the odd cards begin.

1 When your audience is ready, quickly cut your deck into two piles, which you know (but your audience does not) are made up of odd and even cards. It is important to do this smoothly and casually, so that your audience cannot see that you have stacked the deck.

2 Ask a volunteer to shuffle both piles of cards and then choose a pile. Fan out the pile face down and ask them to pick a card and show it only to the audience.

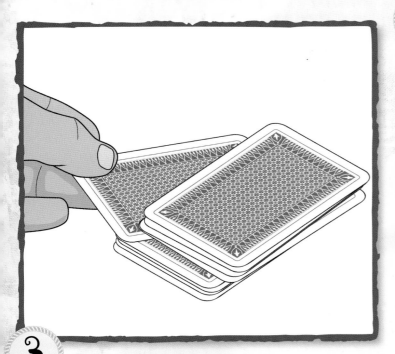

3

Ask them to put their chosen card into the other pile.

4

They can then shuffle this pile as many times as they like.

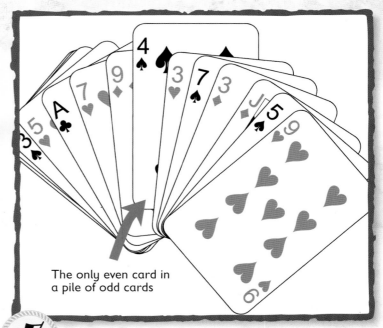

The only even card in a pile of odd cards

5

Take the pile, fan through it and find their card. Your volunteer's chosen card will either be the only odd card among the evens, or the only even card among the odds.

Telling a tale

Some magicians like to use acting and stories to make their tricks seem more exciting to their audience. In the show, Tablo, the Italian magician Gaetano Triggiano performs many different illusions, including sawing a woman in half. The illusions all form part of a story about a man searching for his lost love.

▶ Gaetano Triggiano performs a spectacular card trick during his show, Tablo.

Card peeking

For this trick you will need to master a new skill known as 'card peeking'. This is when you take a quick look at the card on the bottom of the deck, without your audience noticing.

Skills needed...
* Card peeking
* Cutting
* Misdirection

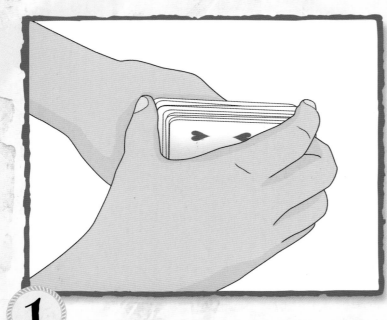

1 Shuffle the cards, remembering to take a quick peek at the bottom card before squaring up the deck.

2 Fan out the cards face down in your hand and ask your volunteer to take one and hold onto it. Square up the deck.

Place new pile on top of the one before

Main deck

3 Place the deck face down on the table and tell your volunteer that you are going to cut the cards into small piles, which you are going to place one on top of the other. Take a small pile off the deck and put it next to the main pile. Repeat this a few times so you end up with five or six small piles.

Top Tip!
Make the cuts small, with just a few cards in each, so that you do not run out of cards before the volunteer puts their card on top in step 4.

4 Ask your volunteer to put their card on top of one of the piles when they feel ready. Then, pick up the main deck and put it top of the pile they choose to put their card on. The card you peeked at earlier is now on top of their card.

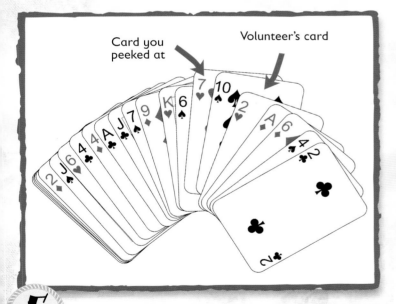

Card you peeked at

Volunteer's card

5 Turn the cards over and fan them out from left to right. Make sure all the cards can be seen. The volunteer's card will be the one to the right of the card you peeked at.

Event magic

Many magicians like to draw attention to their tricks by turning them into large public events. This can be great for escapology tricks – escaping from something – as it can really help to build up the tension.

In 2007, in New York City, USA, the US magician Criss Angel had 24 hours to escape from a metal cube hanging 12 metres above Times Square before it plummeted to the ground. And just to make the trick even more difficult, he had been tied up and the cube lined with a layer of cement.

A large crowd gathered to watch him try to break free. The escape attempt appeared to go wrong when the cube crashed onto the pavement, only for Angel to emerge safe and sound a few moments later!

▼ *Criss Angel looks at the crowds below as he prepares his escape attempt.*

Forcing the cards

The magician places a sealed envelope on a table. They ask a volunteer to choose a card. The volunteer then opens the envelope. Somehow the name of their chosen card has been written on the piece of paper inside!

Skills needed...
* Card forcing
* Stacking the deck

Props needed...
* Envelope
* Paper
* Pen

Preparation

You will need to 'stack the deck', so the third card in the deck is the Queen of Diamonds. Write the name of the card on a piece of paper, put it in an envelope and seal it. Place the envelope in your pocket.

1 Announce to your audience that you have made a prediction about which card your volunteer will choose. Take the envelope from your pocket and place it on the table. You will not touch it again.

2 Give the deck of cards a quick 'false shuffle' and then hand them to your volunteer. Ask them to deal out the top six cards into two rows of three. The Queen of Diamonds should be in the top row on the right-hand side.

3 Ask your volunteer to point to a row.
a) If they point to the top row, take away the bottom row.
b) If they pick the bottom row, also take away the bottom row.
Pretend that their choice helped you to decide which row to remove.

4
Ask your volunteer to pick two cards. If the volunteer picks the first two cards, remove them and the remaining card is their card. Go to step 7.

NEW SKILLS ALERT

Card forcing

You can force someone to pick the card you want them to, whilst making it seem like they have chosen it at random! Once mastered, you can use this skill to make up your own tricks.

5
a) If your volunteer points to the first and the third card, remove the middle card. Go to part b.

b) Ask them to point to another card. Whichever card they choose, remove the first card and give them the card on the right. Go to step 7.

6
a) If the volunteer points to the second two cards, remove the first card. Go to part b.

b) Ask them to point to another card. Whichever card they pick, remove the first card and give them the right-hand card. Go to step 7.

7
Ask your volunteer to turn over their chosen card. Then hand them the envelope, which will reveal your amazing prediction, the Queen of Diamonds.

The pocket

To perform this trick, you will need to wear a jacket with side pockets. You will also have to learn how to do a new piece of 'sleight of hand'.

Preparation

Before you face your audience, take any two cards from the deck of cards and place them out of sight in the right-hand pocket of your jacket.

1 Hand your volunteer the remainder of the deck of cards. Ask them to shuffle the deck, take three cards off the top and lay them face up on the table.

2 Ask the volunteer to silently choose one of the cards.

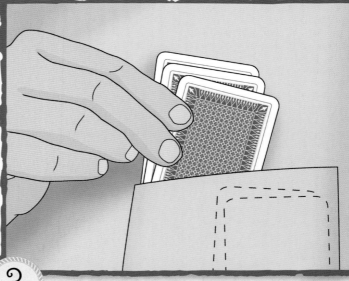

3 Now pick up the three cards. Memorize their order and put them in your right-hand jacket pocket, being sure to keep them separate from the two 'secret' cards already there.

24

Top Tip!

This trick works best if your jacket has large pockets. This will give you enough room to perform the 'sleight of hand'.

4 Ask your volunteer to think of their chosen card. Tell them that you are going to read their mind. After a few moments, say that you think you know what it is and that you are going to get rid of the other two cards.

Popular magician

According to the *Guinness Book of World Records*, more people have seen the magician David Copperfield perform than any other magician. Copperfield has become world famous for his illusions, many involving well-known landmarks. These have included 'levitating over the Grand Canyon' and even 'making the Statue of Liberty disappear'.

▼ *David Copperfield uses his extraordinary skills to levitate a woman.*

5 Reach into your pocket and bring out the two 'secret' cards, keeping the cards chosen by your volunteer safely in your pocket. Place these two cards face down on the table.

6 Ask your volunteer to name their card. When they do, reach into your pocket, count to the correct card and pull it out. The tricky bit is doing this quickly and easily, so that it does not look like you are counting cards in your pocket. This may take a bit of practice.

The vanishing card

This trick requires quite a lot of preparation, but the end result is guaranteed to baffle your audience.

Skills needed…
* Sleight of hand

Props required…
* Handkerchief
* Scissors
* Toothpick or cocktail stick

Preparation

• Using scissors, cut the toothpick so that it is the same length as one of your cards. Remove the sharp ends.

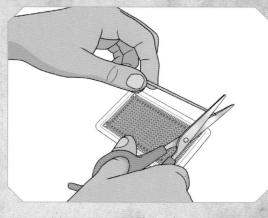

• Tuck the toothpick into the hem of your handkerchief. Make sure it is secure and will not fall out. Place the handkerchief in your pocket.

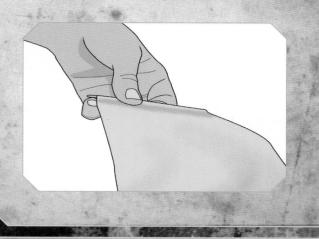

1 Throw a deck of cards onto a table, so that the cards are in a messy pile.

2 Take the handkerchief out of your pocket. Make sure the hem holding the toothpick is facing downwards, so that it cannot be spotted by the audience.

3 Place the handkerchief over the pile of cards. Announce that you are going to make one of the cards disappear.

4 Place your finger and thumb on either end of the toothpick. Pick the toothpick up. To the audience, this will look like you have picked up a card.

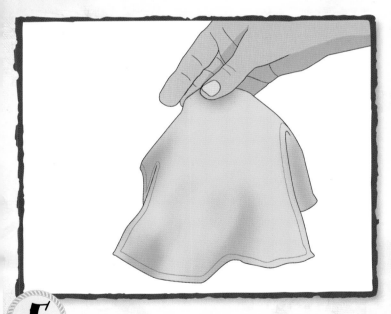

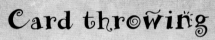

Card throwing

The magician Ricky Jay can throw a playing card more than 60 metres. He can also throw a card with such force that it can pierce the rind of a water melon from more than 3 metres away.

▼ Ricky Jay demonstrates his amazing card skills.

5 Say the magic word, 'abracadabra', lift the hanky in the air and quickly transfer your grip from the toothpick to the corner of the handkerchief. Wave the handkerchief around. It will look like the card has vanished. Only you will know that it was never there to begin with.

The magic shoe

Tricks always seem much more magical if you can find a new and special way to reveal the chosen card.

Preparation
Before facing your audience, peek at the top card of the deck. Write the name of the card on a piece of paper, fold it up, and tuck it in your shoe. Place the handkerchief in your pocket.

1 To get your audience to believe that you are using mixed up cards, perform a quick 'false shuffle'. Then, take the deck and hold it in your right hand just above the table. Put the handkerchief over the deck of cards.

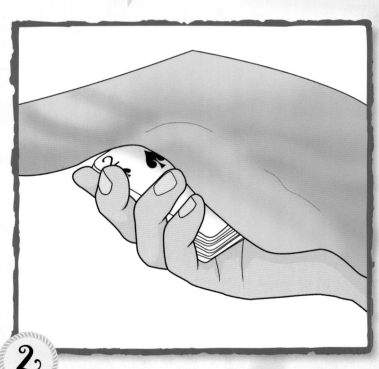

2 As you place the handkerchief over your hand, use your fingers and thumb to turn the deck over so that it is face up. This needs to be done quickly and smoothly, so that your audience does not notice.

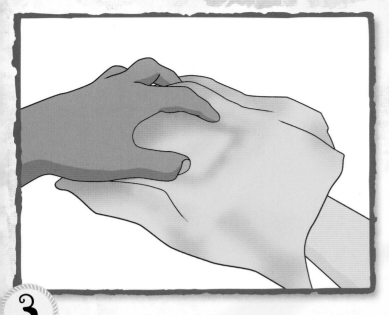

3 Now, ask a volunteer to cut the deck through the handkerchief and to place their pile of cards on the table (still under the handkerchief).

4 Turn the cards in your hand over, so that they are once again face down. The top card will now be the one you looked at earlier. Use your other hand to move your volunteer's pile of cards, so that they cannot inspect it.

5 Give your volunteer the deck of cards in your right hand. Ask them to turn over the top card and say what it is. As they do this, slip off your shoe containing the piece of paper.

6 Ask your volunteer to take the piece of paper out of the shoe and read your prediction. That shoe is magic!

See-through magic

Many magicians perform a trick using cups and balls. However, US magician Jason Latimer performs a special version using see-through glass tumblers. Even though the balls can be seen by the audience at all times, he still manages to make them disappear and reappear – as if by magic.

▶ *Jason Latimer shows his audience that the props are normal before he astounds them with his trick.*

The lift

This trick is simple, but it will probably take a lot of practice before you feel confident enough to try it in front of an audience.

NEW SKILLS ALERT

Double lift

You need to pick up two cards in such a way that it looks like you have only picked up one.

• Use your thumb and first two fingers to find the top two cards.

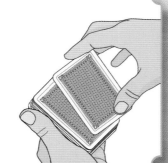

• As you lift the cards press down slightly so that the cards bend a little. The cards will stick together and make it look as if you have only lifted one card.

1 Square up the deck and perform the double lift. Show the card underneath to the audience. They will think that they are looking at the top card.

2 Put the cards back on top of the deck.

3 Now take the top card and put it on the bottom of the deck. The audience will think you are moving the card that they saw.

4 Square up the deck and announce you are going to make the bottom card rise to the top of the pack. Snap your fingers over the deck.

The oldest trick

No one knows how long magic tricks have been around, but it is believed to be many thousands of years. Some archaeologists think that a painting on the wall of a tomb from ancient Egypt shows the earliest image of a magic trick. In the picture, a figure appears to performing an illusion using a series of cups.

▼ *Were these ancient Egyptians performing the cup and ball trick?*

5 Now turn over the top card. It will look to your audience as if the card has 'magically' jumped from the bottom of the deck to the top!

Simple skills to master

In addition to learning the skills mentioned in the 'New Skills Alert' boxes, it is also important to practise the following techniques if you want to become a top magician.

Card counting

For some tricks, the only skill you need is the ability to count – making sure you have laid out or picked up the correct number of cards and then placed them in their correct order.

Card peeking

To 'peek' is to take a secret look at a card, allowing you to memorize its number and suit without your audience realizing what you are doing.

Cutting

To 'cut' a pack is to roughly divide it by taking a pile off the top.

Memory

Having a good memory is vital if you want to be a good magician – tricks often have several stages that need to be remembered clearly and in the correct order.

Observation

A keen eye is one of a magician's most vital skills. You have to be aware of what is going on at all times.

Sleight of hand

You need to be able to move something secretly with your hands in such a way that the audience thinks you are doing something else.

Spelling

For some tricks you will need to spell out a word for the trick to work. Learn how to spell the word – and practise spelling it – before performing the trick or you may make a mistake.

Stacking the deck

Stacking the deck means to secretly arrange the cards, usually before the trick begins, so some of them are in a certain order – which the magician knows, but the audience does not.